Contents

Writing It Right

You Can Write It Right   *4*

   How to Use this Book   *5*

Writing It

Getting Started   *6*

Getting It Right

Revising Drafts   *8*

   Editing and Polishing for Publication   *10*

Getting Grammar Right

How Language Works   *12*

   Parts of Speech   *12*

   Sentences   *13*

Getting Sentences Right

Writing Style   *14*

Sentence Style   *14*

Sentence Sense   *15*

Getting Spelling Right

Spelling Matters   *18*

   How to Be a Better Speller   *18*

Getting Punctuation Right

Proofreading for Punctuation   *22*

   Road Signs for Reading   *22*

SUPPORTING STUDENT WRITERS   *26*

REPRODUCIBLES

Writing Forms   *27*

My Grammar/Usage Checklist   *28*

My Punctuation Checklist   *29*

INDEX   *3 0*

You Can Write It Right

Have you been told that writing is easy? Well, the truth is, it isn't—just ask any writer. Professional writers—people who write for a living—know they need assistance with their work. Sometimes that help comes from resource material, such as books about writing. Sometimes podcast or webcast interviews with other writers can give a writer a new idea, way of thinking about a topic, or look at the whole process of writing. Of course, talking with someone can help you find ideas or shape your writing. But much of the writing you do, you do alone. You can use *Write It Right!* as a companion to guide you through the various stages of your writing.

> "I have been writing books for twenty years. Here's the best thing about it—it is never boring. Here's the worst thing—you write by yourself…"
> — Betsy Byars

This flipbook might help you find a topic and decide on a purpose for your writing. But most of all, it will assist you as you work with your ideas once they are already on the page or on the screen. There are tips to help you make sure your punctuation, spelling, grammar, and other details are accurate so the message you are communicating will be as clear and crisp as possible.

To make all of this come together, you need to get writing ideas and think about your purposes. Then you need to attend to the surface features of your writing—spelling, punctuation, grammar. Most of all, you need time: time to think, consider, wonder, ponder, reflect. And, of course, you need time to write: time to draft your ideas, and time to revise, edit, and polish them. Finally, you need time to put your writing in a form that's suitable for presentation.

How to Use This Book

This is not a book that you have to read from cover to cover. Rather, you can go directly to the pages that deal with a particular need you have at a particular time. If you want a reminder about using commas, if verb tenses are giving you a problem, if you are worried that what you have written might be confusing or ambiguous, then you can refer the appropriate section.

No matter how you use *Write It Right!*, you should be able to find what you need quickly. You might want to start by looking at the index to see what has been included that may be of use to you and where those sections are located. Or you might want to glance through the pages to get a sense of how the handbook is set up, with the tabs at the bottom of the pages showing the main steps or elements of writing.

"Writing is used to clarify thinking."
— Donald Graves

Go ahead and personalize this book for your own needs. As you glance through the pages, or when you're using the book as a reference when you're writing, feel free to attach sticky notes to the sections you find particularly useful, places you want to refer back to, or things you want to ask your teacher about.

In the pages at the back of the book you'll find a way to record the writing forms you've tried or would like to experiment with, and personal checklists for punctuation and usage. Throughout the book are suggestions for keeping track of your writing, and for recording sentences and words you really like or have trouble with.

Use *Write It Right!* to help you produce the best writing you can.

WRITING IT RIGHT

Getting Started

Before and as you write, think about *what* you are writing about, *why* you are writing it, and *how* you can express your ideas.

What to Write: Choosing a Topic

It's usually best to write about what you know—places you've been, experiences you've had, opinions you hold. When you know something about your topic, you can work on how to get your message across to your reader.

Before you start to write, make sure you know enough about your topic:

- make a web of what you want to say, or
- *freewrite*—write whatever comes into your head on your topic.

If your page is full of detail, you're ready to start writing. Once you've chosen a topic, consider what is important to say about it. If your message isn't clear in your own mind, your readers can get confused, too.

Why Write: Considering Your Purpose

Reasons you might have for putting your thoughts and ideas on paper or onscreen include

- to give information; to explain or describe something
- to tell a story; to entertain or amuse others
- to persuade or convince someone
- to tell how you feel about something
- to get someone to respond to your ideas
- to give a voice to ideas that are in your imagination

Spending time sorting out your purpose beforehand will give your writing a sharper focus.

Record It

- Keep a record of the topics that you'd like to write about and have written about.
- Record your purpose so you can refer to it to keep yourself on track as you write.

How to Say It: Choosing a Form

Knowing the purpose for your writing will often determine, or help you determine, the kind of writing and the form it will take.

GIVING INFORMATION (EXPOSITORY WRITING)

Some writing forms are suitable for giving information or expressing ideas or opinions:

- reports
- articles
- interviews
- essays
- letters or opinion pieces
- procedures; e.g., instructions, directions

TELLING STORIES (EXPRESSIVE WRITING)

Some writing forms help to tell a story. The story can be fiction, something that really happened to you (personal narrative), or something that happened to someone else. As well as using the narrative form, try telling your stories through

- journals
- plays
- a series of letters
- song lyrics
- poetry

MAKING A STATEMENT

Some writing forms allow you to say what you think or feel in very few words, often using pictures to emphasize the statement:

- buttons
- bumper stickers
- posters
- banners
- captions
- want ads

Choosing and Using a Form of Writing
- Experiment with a form of writing that you don't often use or haven't used before.
- Consider changing one form of writing to another. For example, a personal narrative might become a play, a poem, a letter to a friend, or even an article for your school newspaper.

Some forms can be used for many purposes. For example, poetry can be used
- to play with language
- to express thoughts and feelings
- to tell a story
all at the same time!

WRITING IT

Revising Drafts

Revision is the stage in your writing when you make changes to your work that will help make your message *clearer, more meaningful, and more powerful.*

MAKING CHANGES

When you revise, you can change your writing by

1. Adding Information: Sometimes, adding details to your writing can make your message clearer or your writing more interesting.
2. Deleting Information: Deleting unnecessary or unrelated information can emphasize what is most important.
3. Reorganizing Information: Moving words, sentences, or even whole paragraphs can sometimes help your reader follow the flow of your ideas more easily.
4. Rewriting: Often as you revise, you get a better idea—a new topic, a different focus, another way of expressing yourself. You might want to start again or rewrite a section.

When you are revising your work, you will be asking yourself a lot of questions. The checklist here can guide you:

Revision Checklist

The Message
☐ Will my readers understand what I am saying; that is, does my writing have a purpose and a focus?
☐ Have I stated my main ideas clearly? Do I get my point across?
☐ Are there any ideas that don't support my main ideas and so should be removed? Have I included ideas that might confuse the reader and so should be taken out?
☐ Have I included everything that I wanted or needed to say? Have I said too much?

The Organization
☐ Are events in an order that makes sense?
☐ Are the ideas expressed in a logical sequence?

The Words
☐ Do the words I've used express the meaning I want to convey?
☐ Would other words express my meaning more clearly?
☐ Is my writing both clear and interesting?

"Hearing" What You've Written

When you revise your writing, you try to hear or read it as your audience might. Here are some ideas to help you take a fresh look at your writing:

- Read what you've written to yourself. Get your ideas off the page by reading them so you can *hear* the words in your head.
- Read your work aloud.
- Read your work to someone and ask for their questions and comments. You don't have to use the suggestions other people give you, but they might point out where your writing isn't clear, or suggest things you hadn't thought about.
- Ask someone to read your writing to you. As a listener, you will be able to get a sense of how your writing sounds, and hear which words, phrases, sentences, and paragraphs need your attention.
- Make a sound recording of you reading your work, and play it back. Listen to hear if the writing flows from one idea to the next and "hangs together."
- Put your writing away for a while, then come back to it. Often, just setting your writing aside for a day or two will help you see it in a new way.

FINDING YOUR WRITER'S VOICE

Just as you can hear the difference between the sounds made by a trumpet and by a piano, differences in the "sound" of writing can also be identified. Your writing is different from anyone else's because you have your own way of expressing yourself.

Your writing voice has to do with the words you use and the way you use those words. Your writing will be more meaningful, more interesting, and more authentic if you write it in your own voice, so it's worth getting a sense of your writing voice and developing it.

The best way to find your writing voice is to write a lot. Read aloud what you write and listen to its sound. You'll start to be able to tell how your own writing voice is different from the writing voices of others.

Revision takes time, but it's time well spent if you carefully review what you've written. Use a variety of sources and resources to help you: dictionary, thesaurus, Internet, other people. Revision is not something you can do well on your own. It's a collaborative effort!

Editing and Polishing for Publication

You will write for many reasons and in many forms. In some cases, you will keep your writing to yourself—for example, when you write a diary or journal entry, notes or observations, or early writing drafts. However, often when you write, you know that others—your classmates, a teacher, or family members—are going to read your work. When you write something that someone else is going to read, you want it to be the best it can be.

Editing is the stage in writing when you proofread for spelling, punctuation, and rules or conventions of language usage that help to make your message clearer for your readers. If you answered "yes" to all the questions in the Clarity Checklist, you are ready to go on to editing your writing.

Publishing Your Writing

Often, you put effort into your writing—revising for meaning, editing to help make your meaning clear to your readers—to get your writing ready for an audience. Publishing your writing simply means sharing it with someone else. Sharing can be as small as reading a story to a friend, or as large as putting your writing on a website for the whole world to see.

Here are some ways that you can share your writing with others:

- Read your story to a classmate, friend, or family member. Invite an oral response.
- Send your writing in a letter to a friend by snailmail or e-mail. Invite a written response.
- Make a collection of your stories or poems. Include a cover, table of contents, illustrations. Throw it up on the class website.
- Create a newspaper on the wall in your classroom (using a large piece of Bristol board) or online. Display articles, reports, cartoons, jokes, puzzles. Change the displays regularly and frequently to keep the "news" current.

- Rehearse and make a sound recording of a story or poem, adding sound effects. Add the sound clip to the listening area of your class web page, send it to someone by e-mail, or share it as a download.
- Write stories and poems for a special audience—e.g., a class of younger children, hospital patients, senior citizens.
- Submit your writing to the school's newsletter for school community reading.
- Display your writing on a classroom or school bulletin board. Invite feedback from classmates as well as from teachers.
- Write and send letters and e-mails—to the editor of your local newspaper, to authors telling them how you feel about their books, to organizations for information for projects, to guests to invite them and thank them for coming to the class.
- Publish your writing on your class blog/website for your classmates and others around the world to read.

Keep a record of your published work, including its form (e.g., prose, poem, play, report) and the date you shared it.

GETTING IT RIGHT

How Language Works

To be a good writer, you have to understand how your language works. Here are some terms and tips to help you.

Parts of Speech

NOUNS

A noun is a part of speech used to name a person, place, thing, or abstract concept. There are ways of categorizing nouns.

Common or Proper

Common nouns name a general person or place: e.g., *man*, *city*. *Proper nouns* name a specific person or place: e.g., *David Suzuki*, *Vancouver*. A proper noun usually begins with a capital or upper case letter.

Singular or Plural

Nouns can be *singular* (referring to one) or *plural* (referring to more than one). Many nouns are made plural by adding *-s* or *-es* to the end or, if the singular ends with a *y*, changing the *y* to *i* and then adding *-es*. However, there are exceptions: child/children; moose/moose; turkey/turkeys.

Nouns in Sentences

A singular noun or pronoun takes a singular verb: e.g., *The boy* is *playing in the schoolyard*. A plural noun takes a plural verb: *The boys* are *playing in the schoolyard*.

PRONOUNS

Pronouns are used in place of nouns, and help to avoid repetition. Compare these two sentences (both are correct):

> When *Kim* got home, *Kim* called *Kim's* best friend.
> When *Kim* got home, *she* called *her* best friend.

Repetition makes the first sentence more difficult to read.

Using the Right Pronoun

Trying to decide which pronoun to use?

> They invited Sam and *me.* (or is it "Sam and *I*"?)
> Carson and *I* (or *me*?) went to the party.

Say the sentence without the noun and the word *and*. Use the form that sounds right:

> They invited (Sam and) *me.*
> (Carson and) *I* went to the party.

VERBS

Verbs often provide or describe the action in a sentence:

I *auditioned* for the band. I *play* drums. I *will be performing* next week. *Will* you *come* to hear me?

Verb Tense

In the first sentence, the action happened in the past. The verb in the second sentence tells the reader that the action is happening in the present. And in the last two sentences, the action will happen in the future. The verb tense signals to your reader when things happen.

ADJECTIVES

An adjective *modifies* (describes) or gives more information about a noun or pronoun:

A *foreign* car was parked on the *deserted* street.

Adjectives can make a more detailed and exact picture in the reader's mind. But don't get carried away. Sometimes, one strong adjective is better than a long string of adjectives.

ADVERBS

Adverbs *modify* (describe) verbs. Like adjectives, they help the reader see a better picture of what the writer is trying to say. Many adverbs end with the letters "ly":

The car moved *slowly* down the road.

Sentences

A sentence expresses a complete thought. Sentences usually have two parts: a *subject* (what the sentence is about) and a *predicate* (what the subject does or what happens to the subject). Subjects are usually nouns or pronouns; predicates are usually verbs.

Subject	Predicate
He	is a good dancer.
The end of the story	puzzled me.

Grammar "Fumblerules"

These "fumblerules" are examples of the problems they describe.

- Verbs has to agree with their subjects. (See page 12)
- Don't switch verb tenses unless it was necessary. (See page 13)
- Check for run-on sentences, those are sentences that run on and on and are linked together with the word *and* or a comma and that tire the reader. (See page 16)
- No sentence fragments. (See page 15)
- It should refer to a noun used earlier. (See page 16)
- Use apostrophe's correctly. (See page 22)
- Avoid commas, that are not necessary. (See page 24)
- Write adverbs correct. (See page 13)
- Writing carefully, dangling words can be avoided. (See page 16)
- And finally, proofread carefully to see if you any words out. (See page 10)

GETTING GRAMMAR RIGHT

Writing Style

The way you select your clothes, style your hair, and so on, creates your personal fashion style. In the same way, how you choose and use words and sentences creates your individual writing style. Writing style depends on

- **what** you're writing about (the subject): e.g., if you're writing an information piece, your writing will be more focused and to the point.
- **whom** you're writing for (the audience): e.g., if you're writing for a young audience, your sentences will be shorter, as will word length.
- the **tone** of your writing: e.g., if you're creating a happy tone, you'll try for a "breezy" style; if you're writing a letter to the editor to express disappointment or anger, you'll use a more clipped, tighter style.

Sentence Style

Sentence style refers to the different ways that sentences can keep the reader interested. Here are some ways to "write with style."

- Vary the length of sentences.

  The air was crisp and cool. The geese, flying in their standard V formation, made their way south. Fall was coming.
- Vary sentences by using different kinds of words to begin sentences.

You can start sentences with
- adverbs
- phrases such as "With caution…," "As quickly as possible…," "Knowing the answer…"
- link words (see chart below)

Link Words

Some link words join words or ideas of the same importance:

and	or	yet	but	nor	so

Some link words show a connection in meaning between two sentences:

besides	therefore	indeed	otherwise
consequently	however	moreover	

Some link words are used in pairs:

either…or	not only…but also
neither…nor	both…and

Some link words join words or ideas in which one idea is less important than or dependent on the other:

after	if	unless	wherever
although	since	until	while
as	though	when	who
because	till	where	whom
before			

- Vary the order of parts of sentences to highlight important information.

> Priya will not attend the meeting unless the agenda is changed.
> *Unless the agenda is changed*, Priya will not attend the meeting.

- Incorporate new ideas into your original sentence to add detail.

> This was the day of the championship baseball game.
> *After a grueling, three-month season*, this was the day of the championship baseball game.

Writing Stylish Sentences

- Look at how published writers vary their sentences.
- Watch for and record sentences that use interesting words, are unusual, or communicate a message clearly.

- Combine two short sentences by using link words.

> The family picnic is today. It is raining.

These sentences can be combined because the ideas in each are linked. The choice of link word can change the meaning (see the chart on page 14).

> The family picnic is today **and** it is raining. (statement of fact)
> The family picnic is today **but** it is raining. (*Will they still have the picnic?*)
> The family picnic is today **although** it is raining. (*They'll have the picnic anyway.*)

Sentence Sense

If a statement makes sense on its own, it is likely a good sentence. To find and correct problems with sentence structure, reread your writing carefully and really *listen* to what you've written. If you sense that something is wrong, it might be due to one of these common problems with sentence structure.

SENTENCE FRAGMENTS

A sentence fragment is an incomplete sentence that is punctuated like a complete sentence. Sentence fragments are usually missing a subject or a predicate.

> Leaving the cave. Liz hurried up the stairs.

You find yourself asking, "*Who* left the cave?" The first sentence is missing a subject. It needs to be combined with the full sentence:

> Leaving the cave, Liz hurried up the stairs.

Writers sometimes use sentence fragments in dialogue, where the give and take of conversation makes the meaning clear. Command sentences often have just a verb, since the subject (*you*) is understood by the reader. But unless you're sure sentence fragments are not making your writing confusing, you should avoid them.

For a review of terms like *subject*, *predicate*, *modifying words*, *noun*, *pronoun*, and *verb*, see Getting Grammar Right starting on page 12. For a review of punctuation, see Getting Punctuation Right starting on page 22.

RUN-ON SENTENCES

Run-on sentences occur when you don't use enough periods or when you combine two sentences incorrectly. Don't let this happen to you!

> The boy ran into the room to get his books for school and he was late and the history test he had studied so hard for was being given in the first period and he only had twenty minutes to get to school and he didn't think he would make it on time.

It's better to take out some of the *and*s and make several sentences. Your readers will be able to stop along the way, catch their breath, and have time to see and think about the pictures being made by your words.

> The boy ran into the room to get his books for school. He was late. The history test he had studied so hard for was being given in the first period and he only had twenty minutes to get to school. He didn't think he would make it on time.

"DANGLING" WORDS AND PHRASES

Modifying (or describing) words or phrases that don't clearly describe another word in the sentence are sometimes said to *dangle*.

The result of dangling modifiers can be sentences that are unclear or even unintentionally funny:

> She wants to play baseball *badly*.
> Enclosed is an article about a woman who had quadruplets *in the envelope*.

The "cure" for dangling words or phrases is usually to move them closer to the words they modify or describe:

> She *badly* wants to play baseball.
> Enclosed *in the envelope* is an article about a woman who had quadruplets.

UNCLEAR PRONOUNS

Before you use a pronoun in place of a noun, be certain you have already used the noun.

> Does this sentence make sense?

> John took *it* out of his pocket and put *it* on the table.

To what does *it* refer? You can make the meaning clearer by using a noun to identify the object, and then using a pronoun in its place:

> John took *his wallet* out of his pocket and put *it* on the table.

If you mean two different objects, use two nouns:

> John took *his wallet* out of his pocket and put *the money* on the table.

SUBJECT–VERB AGREEMENT

With a singular subject, you use a singular verb; with a plural subject, a plural verb—that is, the subject and verb should agree. For example:

I was late for the game.
They were late for the game.

When choosing a verb, you can usually rely on what sounds right to you. This chart shows some troublesome subjects with correct examples.

Troublesome Subjects

Subject	Examples
Each (one)/everyone/ someone (singular)	*Each* of the volunteers *has* a job to do. *Everyone is* going to the school game. *Someone is* trying to reach you.
Either (one)/neither (one) (singular)	*Either* of the players *is* a good choice. *Neither* of the boys *wants* to go.
Nobody/everybody/ somebody (singular) • *-body* is singular	*Nobody* likes me. *Everybody* hates me. *Somebody is* watching.
Collective nouns (sometimes singular, sometimes plural)	*The class is* visiting the museum. (singular) More *people are* renting DVDs than going to movie theatres. (plural)

SWITCHES IN VERB TENSE

Consider what happens when verb tenses are mixed:

John *takes* the money out of his wallet and *gave* it to his father.

The first verb *takes* is in present tense—John is doing it now. The second verb *gave* is in past tense—John did it in the past. The reader gets confused because the sentence sounds as if John gave the money to his father before he took it out of his wallet. And, of course, that isn't what the writer meant. Consider this:

John took the money out of his wallet and gives it to his father.

Again, there's confusion because the verb tenses are mixed: *took* (past) and *gives* (present). The sentences can be rewritten either in present tense or past tense:

John takes the money out of his wallet and gives it to his father.
John took the money out of his wallet and gave it to his father.

Sentence Checklist

When you are proofreading sentences for "sense," make sure
☐ the subjects and verbs agree
☐ you used a consistent verb tense
☐ you don't have run-on sentences
☐ you check for sentence fragments
☐ your pronoun references are clear
☐ you used a variety of sentence types

GETTING SENTENCES RIGHT

Spelling Matters

See if you have trouble reading this passage:

> fi yuo cna raed tihs, yuo hvae a sgtrane mnid too! Cna yuo raed tihs? Olny 55 plepoe out of 100 can. I cdnuolt blveiee taht I aulaclty uesdnnatrd htis.

If you did, try reading this:

> If you can read this, you have a strange mind too! Can you read this? Only 55 people out of 100 can. I couldn't believe that I actually understand this.

Both examples are sending the same message to the reader, but the second paragraph is easier to read because it was written using *standard* or *conventional spelling*. Imagine trying to read a whole book written like the first example!

Spelling words correctly is a courtesy to readers because it allows them to focus on the meaning of what you have written, rather than on trying to figure out what the words are supposed to be.

How to Be a Better Speller

Some questions to ask yourself that may help you spell correctly:

DOES IT LOOK RIGHT?

When you've written a word you're not sure you've spelled correctly, try writing it with another spelling. Which spelling "looks right" to you? For example, is it *mocasin* or *moccasin*? If you chose *moccasin*, you're right.

Keep a list of words that you have trouble spelling, including how you spelled the word and the correct spelling.

ARE YOU PRONOUNCING THE WORD CORRECTLY?

Say the word *February*. If you pronounce it "Febuary," you'll probably leave out the *r* in the middle of the word. For longer words, divide the word into syllables as you say it; e.g., *de-mon-stra-tion*. When you say the word more slowly and divide it into syllables, you can hear the sounds better and that might help you spell the word.

Some words that are often mispronounced and, therefore, often misspelled: temperature (*tempature*), chocolate (*choclate*), Wednesday (*Wendsday*), surprise (*suprise*), separate (*seprate*), Antarctic (*Antartic*), athlete (*athalete*), ask (*aks*), kindergarten (*kindegarden*), prescription (*piscription*), interesting (*inneresting*), escape (*excape*), federal (*fedral*), foliage (*folage*), height (*heighth*), library (*liberry*), sherbet (*sherbert*), verbiage (*verbage*), listening (*lisning*), raspberry (*razberry*), probably (*probly*)

Many of these spelling errors would be helped with the correct pronounciation—er, *pronunciation*!

Memorizing the rule "*i* before *e* except after *c*" will help you to spell *grief* and *belief*, as well as *receive* and *ceiling*. But you'll have to remember that *neighbor* and *weigh* are exceptions to the rule. Sometimes rules can help, but most rules have exceptions.

Two of the most commonly misspelled words are *recommend* and *accommodate*. For words like these, you can make up your own rule for remembering which one has two *c*'s and two *m*'s; for example, "*Accommodate* is such a long word that it can accommodate two *c*'s and two *m*'s."

If you know most of the letters in the word, then the best way to make certain that your spelling is correct is to use a dictionary. Remember: when you find what you think is the correct spelling, read the definition to make sure you haven't selected a word that has a similar spelling; for example, *idle* and *idol*.

There are other ways that you can check your spelling:

- ask your teacher
- ask a friend—but remember to choose someone who is a good speller!
- use spellcheck
- use an online dictionary

1. Pronounce words correctly and enunciate troublesome words carefully. Listen to hear each of the letters and syllables.
2. Pay attention to and keep a list of new words you meet in your reading.
3. Keep a list of words that give you trouble. The more often you see the word spelled correctly, the better your chances are of learning how to spell it correctly without having to look it up. Keeping a personal list of problem words lets you write them correctly and then refer to them as often as you need to.
4. When you're reading and come to a word that you have trouble spelling, stop and take a closer look. Add it to your personal spelling list for future reference.

Some Frequently Misspelled Words

Word	Note that…
wiener	…the *i* comes before the *e*, even though you expect the *e* to come first since it is the vowel that is sounded.
vegetable	…we don't hear the *e* in the middle of the word.
often	…some people don't pronounce the *t*.
a lot thank you	…written as two words, not one.
temperature	…most people don't pronounce the *a*.

More Words that Give Writers Trouble!

absence	guarantee	magazine	principal	stationery
all right	gymnasium	mechanic	principle	statue
aluminum		medicine	privilege	succeed
athletics	handkerchief	mischievous	proceed	syllable
	height	misspelled	professor	
beautiful		mosquito	professional	technique
beginning	idle	muscle	pursue	thermometer
business	idol	mystery		tomorrow
	interference		quiet	tragedy
calendar	intrigue	necessary	quotient	
cemetery	irresponsible	neither		unconscious
chocolate	interrupt	niece	realize	unique
cocoa		nickel	receipt	
cough	jealousy	nuisance	recipe	vacuum
	judgment		recommend	vicious
desert		occasion	restaurant	
dessert	knowledge	occur	rhythm	weather
		omission	roommate	whether
efficient	laboratory	orchestra		weird
embarrass	leisure		sandwich	
escape	library	parallel	schedule	
excellent	lightning	permanent	science	
	likable	physician	secretary	
fatigue	loose	possess	separate	
foreign	lose	precede	souvenir	
	luxury	preferred	stationary	

Frequently Confused

IT'S *AND* ITS

- *It's* is the contraction for *it is*: *It's* still raining.
- *Its* shows possession or ownership: The dog buried *its* bone.

Example of both usages:

The Outdoor Education Centre School has *its* good side—*it's* outside!

> *Its* is the only word in the English language that drops the apostrophe when it is possessive. And there's no such spelling as *its'*!

THERE, THEIR, *AND* THEY'RE

- *There* indicates a place: Put the book *there*.
- *Their* indicates possession or ownership: *Their* house is on this street.
- *They're* is the contraction of *they are*: *They're* going to the store.

Example of all usages:

They're going to *their* cottage over *there*.

> *Their* and *there* are pronounced the same way; *they're* is pronounced slightly differently! Can you hear the difference when you say the word? If you can, that will help you with the correct choice and the correct spelling.

TWO, TO, *AND* TOO

- *Two* is a number: There are *two* people.
- *To* indicates direction: I am going *to* the store.
- *Too* can mean *also* or *excessively*: I am going *too*. This box is *too* heavy.

Example of all usages:

Two people is *too* few *to* play baseball.

WHO'S *AND* WHOSE

- *Who's* is the contraction for *who is*: *Who's* the new student in our class?
- *Whose* indicates possession or ownership: *Whose* running shoes are these?

Example of both usages:

I know *whose* mess this is and I know *who's* going to clean it up— and I'm not that person!

YOU'RE *AND* YOUR

- *You're* is the contraction of *you are*: *You're* next.
- *Your* indicates possession or ownership: Is this *your* pencil?

Example of both usages:

Your nose is stuffy. *You're* getting a cold.

> ### Notes on Usage
> - If you can substitute *it is*, then use *it's*; if you can't, then use *its*.
> - If you can substitute *you are*, then use *you're*; if you can't, then use *your*. There's a subtle different in the pronunciation of *your* and *you're*. Can you hear it? If so, it will help you make the correct choice.

GETTING SPELLING RIGHT

Proofreading for Punctuation

Correct punctuation, like correct spelling, is both a courtesy and a help to your reader. Writing that contains no punctuation or is incorrectly punctuated is not only difficult to read, but may also be misunderstood:

> the class was waiting outside the school they were going on a field trip to the museum however the bus hadnt arrived on time so the teacher said lets go back inside and wait in the foyer never thinking that it would be an hour before the bus would arrive

Here's how the writer of the paragraph wanted you to read it:

> The class was waiting outside the school. They were going on a field trip to the museum. However, the bus hadn't arrived on time so the teacher said, "Let's go back inside and wait in the foyer"— never thinking that it would be an hour before the bus would arrive!

Did you find yourself putting in the punctuation as you read? If so, you already know the best way to add punctuation—listen as you read and punctuate as you hear it.

Read these sentences, observing the punctuation marks, and note how the meaning changes.

When I sing well, classmates feel sick./When I sing, well classmates feel sick./When I sing, well, classmates feel sick.

You will be required to work twenty four-hour shifts./You will be required to work twenty-four hour shifts./You will be required to work twenty-four-hour shifts.

Road Signs for Reading

Road signs are there to signal how a driver should travel along the road—stop, yield, go this speed. In the same way, punctuation marks signal to your readers how you want them to travel through a sentence.

THE APOSTROPHE (')

To Show Possession

When you want to show that something belongs to someone or something, use an apostrophe: *Mary's* dress; *the cat's* toy.

When the noun is singular, put the apostrophe before the final *s*: *Peter's* school; the *government's* policy.

When the noun is plural and ends with an *s*, put the apostrophe after the final *s*: the *students'* classroom; their *friends'* advice.

When a plural noun does not end in -*s*, add an apostrophe and an *s*: the *children's* books; the *women's* team.

To Take the Place of Letters

When you want to change two words into one, use an apostrophe in place of the letter or letters you are leaving out:

> we are — we're (the apostrophe takes the place of the *a*)
> they have — they've (the apostrophe takes the place of *ha*)

END PUNCTUATION

End punctuation marks (period, question mark, exclamation mark) signal the end of a sentence. As well, end punctuation changes the way we read a sentence and, therefore, helps us understand the author's intention as to the meaning to be conveyed to the reader.

Although the following sentences contain the same words, the end punctuation changes from sentence to sentence. Look at the end punctuation, then read each sentence in turn, listening for the difference in the way the sentence sounds.

> A storm is coming**.**
> A storm is coming**?**
> A storm is coming**!**

End punctuation is important. It can provide variety to help hold the reader's interest. As you write, think about the end punctuation that will work best to convey the meaning you want your readers to get from your writing.

The Period (.)

Just as the stop sign signals to drivers that they must come to a complete stop before proceeding, a period is used by writers to tell their readers that they must come to a full stop before reading on. Unfortunately, some people don't use enough periods in their writing. The result is that their sentences go on and on (see Run-on Sentences on page 16). And the readers, because they don't get a chance to stop, lose the meaning of what they have just read.

> "To render experience into words is the real business of schools."
> — Dr. James Moffett

The Exclamation Mark (!)

The exclamation mark is another way to signal the end of a sentence:

> I can't believe I ate the whole thing!
> Hurry!
> Don't come any closer!

How do you know when to use an exclamation mark? First you should think about the mood you are trying to create. Exclamatory sentences express strong emotions, such as frustration, surprise, urgency, fear, or anger.

> Come here right now! (urgency)
> The fire's getting closer! (fear)
> I can hardly wait! (excitement)

Read aloud the sentence you've written and listen to your voice. If it is rising and getting louder, use an exclamation mark.

The Question Mark

A question mark is used at the end of an interrogative sentence—a sentence that asks a question—and causes the reader to make a decision by answering the question being asked before going on.

Using End Punctuation
- Mix sentences that need periods, question marks, and exclamation marks to add interest and variety to your writing.
- Don't forget: When you use end punctuation, a capital or upper case letter follows to signal the beginning of the next sentence.

The Comma (,)

Commas are used to signal the reader to pause briefly, but not to come to a full stop. The comma serves several purposes:

- to slow down the reading of a long sentence or one that includes a lot of detail
- to separate items in a date

  Monday, September 12, 2015

- to separate phrases from the rest of the text

  The boy, his spirits dampened, needed to be alone for a while.

Notice that the sentence would still make sense if you removed the phrase *his spirits dampened*.

- to avoid confusion and make the meaning clearer

  Above all, the girls wanted to win the game.

Without the comma, you would read, "Above all the girls…"

- to set off joining words

  The facts, however, didn't support her explanation.

Words like *however*, *therefore*, and *nevertheless* needs book-end commas (one before and one after).

- to set off the salutation in a friendly letter

  Dear Kim,

Using Commas

The best test for the placement of commas is to read the sentence aloud and to listen to when you pause naturally. However, don't use a comma if it will interfere, rather then help, the reader. If in doubt, leave it out!

- to separate the parts of an address or place name

  Winnipeg, Manitoba
  Los Angeles, CA

If you're writing a full address within other text, use commas to separate all the parts of the address:

  Write to me at 203 Main Street, Box #8, Midland, Ontario, L4R 0A3

- to separate words in a list of three or more items:

  Periods, exclamation marks, question marks, commas, and colons are just some of the punctuation marks used by writers.

The Serial Comma

The serial comma precedes the joining word (usually *and* or *or*) in a list of three or more items: I like cats, dogs, and birds.

  The serial comma separates the last two items in a list so they are not read as belonging with each other.

  For lunch we had soup, salad, macaroni, and cheese.
  For lunch we had soup, salad, macaroni and cheese.

Was the cheese separate from the macaroni or was it in the macaroni?

  She took a photograph of her parents, the Prime Minister and the Governor General.
  She took a photograph of her parents, the Prime Minister, and the Governor General.

Were her parents the Prime Minister and the Governor General?

  Using the serial comma is optional—you'll read many lists that don't have it. What is important, however, is that if you use it, you must use it consistently.

Quotation Marks (" ")

Quotation marks always come in pairs, and are used to indicate the exact words that a person says. The first set comes before the first word spoken; the second set immediately follows the last word spoken:

Peter said, "I am going to school."
"I can hardly wait until summer," said Martha, "when I can go swimming again."

Be sure to use quotation marks to separate the speech from the words that tell who is speaking.

Using Quotation Marks

Remember: quotation marks go around the exact words that a person says. The sentence *John said that he was going to school early* doesn't need quotation marks because John's exact words are not used.

Quotation marks are also used to call attention to words that are being used ironically, apologetically, or sarcastically. Consider this sentence: *He shared his "wisdom" with me.* The suggestion is that his words weren't very wise.

The Colon (:)

The colon is not a frequently-used punctuation mark. However, it is important. It is used

- to signal that a list follows

  Remember the class rules: cooperate, help each other, have fun.

- to set off the salutation in a formal business letter

  Dear Ms. Lee:

The Semi-colon (;)

The semi-colon has three main uses:

- to separate two complete and related sentences that have been combined: *The dog is a poodle; the cat is a Siamese.*
- to separate words in a list with commas: *Canada's three largest cities are Toronto, Ontario; Montreal, Quebec; Vancouver, British Columbia.*
- to combine sentences with joining words such as *however, therefore, besides, instead*: *The weather was cold and damp; however, we decided to go on the picnic anyway.*

Note that the semi-colon replaces the first bookend comma (see page 24).

Punctuation Checklist

When you are proofreading for punctuation, make sure you have
- ☐ used a period, question mark, or exclamation mark at the end of a sentence
- ☐ put a capital letter on the first word in a sentence
- ☐ used a comma when it is necessary
  - between words in a series
  - to separate words or groups of words from the rest of the text
- ☐ used quotation marks to set off the exact words of a speaker
- ☐ used apostrophes in contractions or to show ownership or possession
- ☐ used colons and semi-colons correctly:
  - colons to show that a list follows or after the salutation in a formal letter
  - semi-colons to combine two related sentences or to separate words in list when commas are also used

GETTING PUNCTUATION RIGHT

Supporting Student Writers

The most important thing we can give student writers is time—time to think, time to talk with others, time to try writing, time to get feedback along the way, time to revise and edit, time to share late drafts, time to present (publish). Since time is the enemy for many classroom teachers—there's never enough of it—it's important and necessary to identify blocks of time so things can get done.

An Exercise in Punctuation

It's more difficult to write using proper punctuation if we can't hear punctuation as we speak. Give students an unpunctuated paragraph. As they listen, read it to them, emphasizing the punctuation. Then, read it again a little more slowly so students can punctuate as they listen. Have students, as a group/class, read the passage aloud in choral-reading fashion, stating the punctuation as they read.

Mini-lessons: Note the writing challenges that students are facing and offer mini-lessons on those topics: e.g., getting started, sentence variety, paragraphing, punctuation, grammar points.

Conferring: Consider both one-on-one and group conferences. Students can sign up or conferences can be teacher-initiated.

Opportunities for Authenticity: Let students write about what they know about, what they care about, what they talk about, and what others might be interested in reading about. In other words, have students write with with a strong sense of purpose. If students are going to write on topics they know little about and need to research first, have them write in forms and formats they can manage. When students are going to write about topics they know a lot about, that's the time to introduce them to new forms and formats.

Self- and Peer-assessments and -evaluations: Encourage the students to talk about their writing and how they see themselves as writers—what they do well, what they want to work on to become better writers. Encourage pairs to critique each other's work.

Sharing: Give students many opportunities to share their writing and writing ideas throughout the writing process, from the selection of a writing topic to the presentation of a final, polished publication.

Samples and Examples: Give students opportunities to know about different forms and formats for writing by sharing samples and examples with them—but not too many! Too many examples will result in students copying exactly and, while trying out a "template for writing" is good, we don't want students to get so locked into that particular structure that they can't escape.

Encouragement: All writers—young, old, and every age in between—need support and encouragement. Writing is **not** easy!

Writing Forms

Writing Forms I've Tried	Dates																						
Prose																							
advertisement																							
article																							
autobiography																							
biography																							
brochure																							
diary/journal																							
directions/instructions																							
editorial																							
fable																							
historical fiction																							
letter																							
memoir																							
myth/legend																							
personal narrative (true)																							
personal narrative (fiction)																							
report																							
review – book:																							
review – movie:																							
script																							
science fiction story																							
other:																							
Poetry																							
concrete																							
free verse																							
haiku																							
quatrain/cinquain																							
rhymed																							
other:																							

Pembroke Publishers © 2011, *Write it Right* by Ron Benson ISBN 978-1-55138-262-3

My Grammar/Usage Checklist

I need to work on…	Dates					
• varied types of sentences						
• sentence fragments						
• run-on sentences						
• unclear pronouns						
• subject–verb agreement						
• interesting adjectives/adverbs						
• other:						

Pembroke Publishers © 2011, *Write it Right* by Ron Benson ISBN 978-1-55138-262-3

My Punctuation Checklist

I need to work on…	Dates							
• capitals – at the beginning of sentences								
– with proper nouns								
• end punctuation – periods								
– questions marks								
– exclamation marks								
• commas – in a series								
– to separate parts of a sentence								
• colons								
• semi-colons								
• apostrophes – to show possession								
– in contractions								
• quotation marks								
• other:								

Pembroke Publishers © 2011, *Write it Right* by Ron Benson ISBN 978-1-55138-262-3

Index

adding information, 8
adjectives, 13
adverbs, 13
apostrophe, 22
assessment, 26
audience, 14
authenticity, 26

checklists
clarity, 10
checklist, 10
description, 10
colon, 25

clarity
checklist, 10
description, 10
conventional spelling, 18
conferring, 26
common nouns, 12
command sentences, 15
comma, 24
serial, 24
using, 24

dangling words and phrases,
16
deleting information, 8
drafts, revising, 8–11

editing, 10
editorial marks, 10
encouragement, 26
end punctuation, 23
using, 23
evaluation, 26
examples, 26
exclamation mark, 23
expository writing, 7
expressive writing, 7

forms
choosing, 7
using, 7
writing, 7, 27
freewriting, 6
"fumble rules", 13

giving information, 7
grammar/usage checklist, 28

incomplete sentences, 15
information
adding, 8
deleting, 8
giving, 8
reorganizing, 8
it's / its, 21

link words, 14

mini-lessons, 26
modifying words, 16

nouns, 12
common, 12
plural, 12
proper, 12
singular, 12

parts of speech
adjectives, 13
adverbs, 13
nouns, 12
pronouns, 12
verbs, 13
peer assessment/evaluation, 26
period, 23
personal narrative, 7
plural nouns, 12
poetry, 7
predicate, 13
pronouns, 12
unclear, 16
using the right, 12
pronunciation, 18
proper nouns, 12
publication
polishing for, 10
writing, 11
punctuation
apostrophe, 22
checklist, 25, 29
colon, 25
comma, 24
correct, 22
end, 23
exclamation mark, 23
exercise in, 26
period, 23
proofreading for, 22–25
question mark, 23
quotation marks, 25
semi-colon, 25
within sentences, 24–25
purpose, 6

question mark, 23
quotation marks, 25
using, 25

reorganizing information, 8
revision
checklist, 8
described, 8
draft, 8–11
publication, 10
run-on sentences, 16

samples, 26
self-assessment/evaluation, 26
semi-colon, 25
sentence fragments, 15
sentences
checklist, 17
combining, 15
command sentences, 15
described, 13
incomplete, 15
incorporating new ideas in, 15
length of, 14
nouns in, 12
predicate and, 13
punctuation within, 24–25
run-on, 16
sense, 15–17
starting, 14
style, 14–15
stylish, 15
subject and, 13
varying order of parts of, 15

serial commas, 24
sharing, 11, 26
singular nouns, 12
spelling, 18–21
conventional, 18
frequently misspelled words, 19, 20
frequently misused words, 21
how the word looks and, 18
improving, 18–19
pronunciation and, 18
remembering and, 19
rules, 19
standard, 18
tips to better, 19
standard spelling, 18
statements, 7
subject–verb agreement, 17
subjects,
sentence and, 13
troublesome, 17
writing style and, 14

their / there / they're, 21
to / too / two, 21
tone, 14
topic
choosing, 6
staying on, 6

usage, 21

verb tense, 13
switches in, 17
verbs, 13
usage, 21
voice, 9

who's / whose, 21
words
commonly misspelled, 19, 20
dangling, 16
frequently confused, 21
link, 14
modifying, 16
pronouncing, 18
remembering how to spell, 19
spelling, 18–21
usage, 21
writer's voice, 9
writing
audience and, 14
changing, 8
choosing a form of, 7
expository, 7
expressive, 7
forms of, 7
hearing your, 9
publishing, 11
sharing, 11
subject and, 14
supporting, 26
taking a fresh look at, 9
tone of, 14
what to write, 6
why to write, 6
writing style
audience, 14
sentence sense, 15–17
sentence style, 14–15
subject, 14
tone, 14

you're / your, 21